WHAT DO THEY DO?
JUDGES

BY JOSH GREGORY

CHERRY
LAKE
Publishing

Published in the United States of America by Cherry Lake Publishing
Ann Arbor, Michigan
www.cherrylakepublishing.com

Content Adviser: Honorable James F. Holderman, Chief Judge, United States District Court, Northern District of Illinois
Reading Adviser: Cecilia Minden-Cupp, PhD, Literacy Consultant

Photo Credits: Cover and page 1, ©Marmaduke St. John/Alamy; page 5, ©iStockphoto.com/junial; page 7, ©iStockphoto.com/LifeJourneys; page 9, ©iStockphoto.com/thelinke; page 11, ©Image Source Black/Alamy; page 13, ©Huaxiadragon/Dreamstime.com; page 15, ©Gerard1723/Dreamstime.com; page 17, ©Ilene MacDonald/Alamy; page 19, ©Jason Maehl, used under license from Shutterstock, Inc.; page 21, ©Junial/Dreamstime.com

LIBRARY OF CONGRESS CATALOGING-IN-PUBLICATION DATA
Gregory, Josh.
  What do they do? Judges / by Josh Gregory.
    p. cm.—(Community connections)
  Includes bibliographical references and index.
  ISBN-13: 978-1-60279-807-6 (lib. bdg.)
  ISBN-10: 1-60279-807-9 (lib. bdg.)
  1. Judges. 2. Judges—United States. I. Title. II. Series.
  K2146.G74 2010
  347.73'14023—dc22   2009042803

Cherry Lake Publishing would like to acknowledge the work of The Partnership for 21st Century Skills. Please visit *www.21stcenturyskills.org* for more information.

Printed in the United States of America
Corporate Graphics Inc.
July 2010
CLFA07

JUDGES

CONTENTS

WHAT DO THEY DO?

WHAT IS A JUDGE?

A police officer walks to the front of the courtroom. "All rise for the Honorable Judge Smith," he says.

Everyone stands up. A person in long black robes walks into the room. The person sits behind a tall desk called a **bench**. It's the judge!

A judge sits behind a bench while hearing a case.

Judges are an important part of the **legal system**. They need to know the law. They decide how laws are used.

They also hear court cases. They decide what should happen to **criminals** who are proven guilty.

Judges listen to lawyers as they argue their cases.

THINK!

Most judges used to work as lawyers. Why do you think this is? Do lawyers and judges need to know many of the same things?

Judges' decisions can change many people's lives. It is important for judges to be fair. They must think carefully about every case they hear. This makes being a judge a hard job.

Judges often discuss laws and cases with one another.

PASSING JUDGMENT

Judges work in courtrooms during a **trial**. They use **gavels** to get everyone's attention.

They make sure the trial is fair. They make sure the lawyers follow the rules. A judge can send people to jail when they do not obey the law.

A judge bangs a gavel to bring quiet to a courtroom.

There are many TV programs that show court trials. Watch the judge the next time you see one of these shows. How are TV judges different from real-life judges? How are they alike?

Laws change all the time. Judges need to keep up with these changes. They study law books. They review other cases. They learn what other judges decided.

Some judges write down what they know about the law. Lawyers and other judges use this information in their own work.

Lawyers often read about decisions that judges have made.

Some judges are **elected** to office. Others are **appointed**. They must show that they can do a good job. People will not vote for judges who are unfair.

Some judges run for office and are elected by voters.

15

DIFFERENT KINDS OF JUDGES

Judges work on many cases. Some hear cases about business or family issues. Others work on criminal cases.

Some judges work only in one city. Others work for a state. **Federal** judges hear cases that affect the whole country.

Judges listen as lawyers ask questions during a trial.

The most powerful judges in the United States are the **justices** on the U.S. **Supreme Court**. This court hears only the most important cases.

The president appoints Supreme Court justices. Most serve for the rest of their lives.

Justices of the U.S. Supreme Court work in this building.

A federal judge works on cases across states. For example, someone could commit crimes in more than one state. Maybe someone in New York uses the Internet to commit a crime in California. Can you think of other cases a federal judge might hear?

19

Judges try to make sure that the law is fair for everyone. They help keep criminals off the streets. They also help keep people who are innocent from going to jail.

Next time you see a judge, think about all the things they do. Maybe one day you could be a judge, too!

A judge considers all the information before deciding a case.

GLOSSARY

appointed (uh-POIN-tid) given a job by an official

bench (BENCH) the desk a judge sits behind when he or she is in a courtroom

criminals (KRIM-uh-nuhlz) people who break the law

elected (i-LEK-tid) chosen by voters

federal (FED-ur-uhl) having to do with the government of the whole nation

gavels (GAV-uhlz) small mallets used to call for quiet

justices (JUHSS-tiss-iz) judges

legal system (LEE-guhl SISS-tuhm) the system that makes sense of and enforces laws

supreme court (suh-PREEM KORT) the most powerful court in a country or state

trial (TRYE-uhl) the process of deciding the outcome of a case

FIND OUT MORE

BOOKS

Gorman, Jacqueline Laks. *Judge*. Pleasantville, NY: Weekly Reader, 2008.

Harris, Nancy. *What's the State Judicial Branch?* Chicago: Heinemann Library, 2008.

Harris, Nancy. *What's the Supreme Court?* Chicago: Heinemann Library, 2008.

WEB SITES

Supreme Court of Canada
www.scc-csc.gc.ca/court-cour/ju/index-eng.asp
Read about the court and its justices.

Time for Kids—A Look at the Supreme Court
www.timeforkids.com/TFK/specials/articles/0,6709,1103946,00.html
Learn more about the U.S. Supreme Court.

INDEX

24

ABOUT THE AUTHOR

Josh Gregory writes and edits books for children. He lives in Chicago, Illinois. Thankfully, he has never been on trial.